YOUR KNOWLEDGE HAS VALUE

Bibliographic information published by the German National Library:

The German National Library lists this publication in the National Bibliography; detailed bibliographic data are available on the Internet at http://dnb.dnb.de .

Imprint:

Copyright © 2019 GRIN Verlag
Print and binding: Books on Demand GmbH, Norderstedt Germany
ISBN: 9783668917033

This book at GRIN:

https://www.grin.com/document/458146

Julian Schoenemeyer

The munitions of terroristic attacks in Europe

GRIN Verlag

GRIN - Your knowledge has value

Since its foundation in 1998, GRIN has specialized in publishing academic texts by students, college teachers and other academics as e-book and printed book. The website www.grin.com is an ideal platform for presenting term papers, final papers, scientific essays, dissertations and specialist books.

Visit us on the internet:

http://www.grin.com/

http://www.facebook.com/grincom

http://www.twitter.com/grin_com

The munitions of terroristic attacks in
Europe

Table of contents

1. How can we stay ahead of a terrorist's arsenal?

The aim of this paper is to present and outline the munitions terrorists in Europe are using in order to harm innocent people. From the recent terrorist attacks in Europe we know that they were very lethal and we must stay updated about their arsenal in order to prepare our defensive against those different kinds of weapons. Therefore, I have got the following thesis that needs to be proven.

The arms of terrorists who are targeting Europe have changed in the 21st century.

The purpose of this paper is to analyse if the weaponry of terrorists in Europe has changed within the 21st century and to prepare better against those new threats. In order to approach this thesis statement, it is important to ask the right research question for that. The question is:

What munitions are terrorists in Europe using today and did they change since the beginning of the 21st century?

In order to answer this question, I will analyse the terrorist attacks in the recent years and find out what weapons the terrorists have used. Then I will count how often the different weapons were used in the attacks and compare them to each other. Then, it must be examined, if there is a rising number of a special kind of weapon that was not so often used before the year 2000.

Based on this research, I can point out my hypothesis:

If we know what arms the European extremists are using for their attacks nowadays beforehand, we can prevent those attacks better.

In order to question this hypothesis some specific scientific methods are used in this paper. Foremost, a quantitative research approach is used in order to rank how often what type of munition was used in a recent terroristic attack. As a basis for the data of the different incident's articles from the newspapers USA today and Süddeutsche Zeitung are examined. They list all the recent attacks in a chronological order and it offers also an insight what type of munitions was used by the terrorists. From there, hard empirical data can be generated. In addition, a table will be created in order to quantify the number of the arms that were used. To answer the posed research question the numbers have to be compared to each other at the end.

But before we can start to examine the different weapons, we have to categorise them first. Therefore, the book of Cindy Combs, `Terrorism in the Twenty First Century´, is very helpful.

2. How can the weaponry of a terrorist be categorised?

Firstly, each arm has to be carefully put into a category in order to examine how often a weapon from each category is used in the 21st century. To do this, we should focus on the categories that Cindy Combs has given us in her book.

The first category of munitions we think about in our mind when it comes to terrorism are explosives. But what types of explosives are available to a terrorist? According to Cindy Combs, many explosives are homemade devices with a focus on a big blast rather than being a conventional bomb. (Combs, 2017) That allows the terrorists to smuggle them into airplanes because metal detectors are useless against them. In addition those handmade explosives can be easily assembled locally at the terrorists home. (Combs, 2017) It should also be pointed out that one can count a fully fuelled airplane as an explosive device as well as a truck that is loaded with flammable chemicals and explosive material in order to trigger a blast. (Combs, 2017) Terrorists are also very efficient to do a lot of damage by using only small amounts of explosives. Combs named this method the so called `shaped-charge principle´. (Combs, 2017) That means that terrorists are `*focusing the force of the explosion in a desired direction´* (Combs, 2017, p.163) A new type of bomb should also be added to the category of explosives. The newly emerged so called improvised explosive device (IED). This kind of explosive device can be described as `*a homemade bomb, designed to maim or kill an enemy, typically thrown or left concealed on the side of a road´* (Combs, 2017, p. 163) Those devices are easy to manufacture and the terrorist can get the components from a local hardware shop. That makes IED´s widely accessible for a wide range of potential terrorists. They can be thrown at a target or triggered by a civil device like a cell phone. (Combs, 2017) This makes them also very easy to handle.

Secondly, the category of assassinations and ambushes have to be added to our list. They can also be a kind of munition against innocent people. Terrorists are choosing their targets who they want to assassinate very wisely. Because of their publicity and symbolic value politicians can be a very interesting target to aim for. The terrorists are doing this in a long and detailed planning phase in order to surprise the victim and to secure the execution. (Combs, 2017)

Thirdly, the destructive potential of small firearms shouldn´t be underestimated and they can be identified as another category of munition. Under this category one can find pistols, rifles and sawed-off shotguns. (Combs, 2017) Terroristic groups who lack capital like them because they are low in purchase costs and they are easy to handle as well. A long training process is no longer needed. They are also easily to obtain because of the loose gun regulation laws in many countries. (Combs, 2017)

The fourth category of munitions that has to be considered are automatic weapons. Those arms are the preferred ones under terrorist groups for several reasons. They are highly available to them as well as easy to hide. Moreover, they have a high rate of fire and they are dealing a devastating psychological harm to the targets like civilians or security forces. (Combs, 2017) Assault rifles and submachine guns are the most widespread types of this category (Combs, 2017) The most popular assault rifles amongst terrorists is the AK-47 that was easily accessible after the demise of the Soviet Union. Terrorists like it because of the durability and the reliability of this automatic weapon. („Why has the AK-47 become the jihadi terrorist weapon of choice? | World news | The Guardian", n. d.) Mark Mastaglio, a UK-based ballistics expert expressed it like this: `It's very easy to use, that's why you see 12-year-olds carrying them. It is tough, it works in all kinds of environments – hot and sandy deserts, or in Siberia. Wherever it is stored it is resilient, and this is why it is so popular. ´ („Why has the AK-47 become the jihadi terrorist weapon of choice? | World news | The Guardian", n. d.)

Portable rockets are marking a fifth category of a terrorists arsenal. This category includes so called precision-guided munitions (PGM´s) that can be explained best in Cindy Combs words, are `devices that can launch missiles whose trajectories can be corrected in flight´ (Combs, 2017, p. 167) These munitions are very harmful because they can even destroy aircrafts and tanks. According to Brian Jenkins, terrorists like the PGM´s because of their widespread military use, high rate of production and they are relatively cheap. (Jenkins, 1978)

A sixth category can be assessed as aerial and naval hijacking. To hijack a civil airplane can generate a lot of public attention on the terrorist group and on their aims. (Combs, 2017) In addition the psychological impact of those skyjacks are devastating even when there are not much casualties. (Combs, 2017) Naval piracy is also rising because of the economic failure in some failing states like Somalia. Piracy has become a well-developed criminal enterprise in some regions and it is a very lucrative business for terrorist groups. (Combs, 2017)

Sabotages and cyber-attacks can be counted as a seventh category. Foremost, western nations with their vulnerable infrastructure are a target of such terroristic activities. (Combs, 2017) By sabotaging the infrastructure terrorists can also disrupt whole governments. When they are able to launch a cyberattack successfully against critical infrastructure, like the power grid, innocent people can also die as a consequence when their basic needs are not satisfied. Those kinds of attacks should be regarded as very dangerous because their damage potential is rising with the widespread of digitalisation.

Another very feared category of munitions is the category of weapons of mass destruction. We count those weapons as the eight category in this research paper. The potential damage of those weapons is devastating and can cost the lives of thousands to millions of casualties. Biological, chemical, radiological and nuclear weapons are falling in this category. (Combs, 2017) Governments and experts are in fear of terrorist groups getting those devastating devices. It is generally assumed that terrorist groups are not able to get their hands on nuclear material to construct a proper working atomic weapon. (Champion & Mattis, 2003) But it is still concerning that the illegal trade of non-fissile nuclear materials rose since the demise of the Soviet Union. (Champion & Mattis, 2003) More dangerous to innocent people are chemical and biological weapons of mass destruction. Terrorists can get them easier than nuclear material and with a little technical expertise they are able to deal tremendous damage within a targeted country. (Champion & Mattis, 2003) Those weapons can also represent symbolic and religious symbols for the terrorists and would have a big impact on the media and on society. (Champion & Mattis, 2003) Even a limited assault with a tiny load of toxic chemicals deployed in a small area of a densely populated city can have tremendous consequences. (Champion & Mattis, 2003) Dr. Champion mentions also that there is a big variety of devices that are capable of delivering the chemical fight substance to the desired target, take for example different kinds of missiles, artillery shells, land mines and bursting smoke devices. (Champion & Mattis, 2003) Biological weapons are also very dangerous because they can be deployed anonymously and can devastate a whole region. (Champion & Mattis, 2003) Their lethal potential is relatively higher compared to chemical and nuclear weapons. Dr. Champion pointed out: `A few kilograms of toxin can be as deadly as a stockpile of chemicals. ´ (Champion & Mattis, 2003, p. 6) There is also the concern that terrorist groups can get their hands on those devastating toxins by infiltrating a laboratory. They could deliver the toxin via spray nozzles on a field or deliver it through an aerosol by using a flying device like a crop duster. (Champion & Mattis, 2003) It is crystal clear by now that a terroristic attack involving weapons of mass destruction is a rising threat to the western world.

The last and one of the most important categories of a terrorists arsenal needs to be pointed out as suicide bombings. Combs describes this new form of terror as an attack `in which an individual carries explosives on his or her person or transport with the intention of detonating himself or herself in an effort to generate casualties among the enemy. ´ (Combs, 2017, p. 175) That amplifies that the terrorist as well as his tool of destruction are transformed into one lethal weapon. They are also very hard to challenge for the security forces because they can't predict where they will strike next. Franco de Masi stated in his book that those suicide bombings have mostly strategic aims like withdrawing enemy forces from an occupied country even if they appear irrational and fanatical at the first glance. (De Masi, 2011) But ideological terrorism plays also a big role in this category. Ideological international terrorism is one of the most dangerous forms of terrorism and has a supranational character. (De Masi, 2011) The martyrs want to create an atmosphere of constant war within a targeted country to trigger vengeance and to turn the attack into a supranational blood bath. (De Masi, 2011) That means, it is very dangerous for western countries to respond to such attacks with bombing a foreign country because this satisfies the demands of the responsible terroristic groups. It is also important to draw a line between nationalist-type of terrorism and global Islamic terrorism, like de Masi distinguished them in their different motivation for suicide martyrs. (De Masi, 2011)

It should also be pointed out that suicide bombing terrorism is a highly efficient and economical munition of a terroristic group. The suicide martyr is even better than a conventional weapon because he doesn't care about his own live and can maximize the inflicted damage by making autonomous decisions. (De Masi, 2011) In addition, suicide bombers do not need to be trained very good and the terrorist group behind it doesn't suffer form a waste of human capital and even the planning of such attacks is easier because there is no need for an escape route. (De Masi, 2011) To put it into a nutshell, suicide bombing is one of the most lethal weapons regarding the output-related costs within the terrorist arsenal compared to the other categories.

Now that the terrorist arsenal is categorised, we can analyse what types of munitions were used in the terroristic attacks that occurred since the year 2000. The different attacks need to be pointed out in order to find out, if there is a special category of weapon that was used more often than others.

The first terror attack that should be examined happened in November 2003 in Turkey. („Timeline", 2016) There are two incidents we should separate from each other. On the 15th of November 2003 two cars packed with explosives and driven by suicide bombers exploded nearby two different targeted synagogues during the sabbath week. („The Synagogue Bombings in Istanbul", 2003) They killed 24 and injured over 300 innocent people. („The Synagogue Bombings in Istanbul", 2003) It was thought that Al-Qaeda was responsible for the attacks because of the detailed planning and the vast amount of explosives involved. („The Synagogue Bombings in Istanbul", 2003) But that was not enough for Turkey. This terroristic attack was followed by another incident on the 20th of November 2003. The second bombing targeted the British consulate and the HSBC bank in Istanbul and was also carried out by suicide bombers with trucks that were loaded with explosives. („Istanbul rocked by double bombing", 2003) The terrorists slayed 27 and injured around 400 people. („Istanbul rocked by double bombing", 2003) Even a British top official was amongst the death, namely general consul Roger Short and the Turkish authorities found al-Qaeda guilty for this strike as well. („Istanbul rocked by double bombing", 2003)

But how can this attack be categorised now? To begin with, the arms that were used in those attacks are pointed out. Both attacks were carried out by suicide bombers using trucks loaded with explosives. Those kinds of weapons are included crystal clear in the 9th category as a very efficient way to carry out a lot of damage. We count both bombings as one big mass suicide bombing for our analysis. In addition, the motivation for those bombings carried out by al-Qaeda can be linked to the global Islamic terrorism that was mentioned before.

Secondly the impact that occurred on March 11th, 2004 needs to be focused. This time, the capital of Spain, Madrid, was the target of the terrorists. („Timeline", 2016) Four commuter trains were struck by a shocking number of ten bombs that were packed with explosives and nails. („The worst Islamist attack in European history", 2007) The bombing hit the trains in a highly frequented time frame in the morning when innocent people were commuting to their workplace. („The worst Islamist attack in European history", 2007) That circumstance made this strike extremely deadly for a lot of people and 191 civilians were killed and another 1800 people were injured. („The worst Islamist attack in European history", 2007) The investigations of the police lead to a van that was packed with remote detonators for the bombs. („The worst Islamist attack in European history", 2007) They found out as well that a group of four young men carried out the attacks and they had links to the terror network al-Qaeda. („The worst Islamist attack in European history", 2007) Further investigations even found a tract that included a strategic demand from the terrorists. They wanted to contribute to the `victory of the Socialist party and the withdrawal of Spanish forces [from Iraq]´ („The worst Islamist attack in European history", 2007 p. 1) A strategic goal can be clearly identified like Franco de Masi pointed out in his book. For examining the weapons that were used we have to take a closer look at the explosives. The ten used bombs were packed with dynamite and deadly enhanced by filling them up with nails to be even more deadly. Moreover, the bombs were triggered remotely through a van nearby. In conclusion the munitions of this horrible attack can be categorised into the first category of this paper under the branch of explosives. To be more specific improvised explosive devices were used in the strike against the trains. The bombs can be clearly characterised as that because the terrorists enriched the deadly device with nails that could be bought from a local hardware shop. The fact that the bombs were triggered remotely form a civilian van strongly supports this statement that the bombs were IED´s as they were defined in the beginning.

Next, the terror attacks of London on the 7th of July are examined. It was one of the worst terror attacks on British soil. Four terrorists with rucksack bombs entered the city of London via train and blew themselves up in three different tube trains and one exploded on a double decker bus. („7/7 attacks", 2015) The suicide bombers killed 52 commuters in total and injured hundreds of innocent people more. („7/7 attacks", 2015) It was found out that the terrorists used also easily available chemicals in order to manufacture the bombs and they put them into ordinary civilian rucksacks. (Ray, 2018) That circumstance makes it very hard for anti-terror units to detect them. It has also to be pointed out that the last detonation didn´t happen in a commuter train because one of the terrorists, namely Hasib Hussain, decided to detonate his bomb on a crowded bus. (Ray, 2018) That might have led to a higher damage potential. Afterwards in September 2005 al-Qaeda deputy leader Ayman al-Zawahiri stated that his terror network was partly responsible for those bloody attacks. (Ray, 2018) In order to fit the munitions of this incident into a category the bombs have to be closer observed. The explosives of the terrorists were homemade from materials that were easily obtainable locally and they were packed into a civilian rucksack. And according to our definition of how inexpensive suicide bombing is the London terror attacks of 2005 have to be fit into category nine. The terrorists did not only carry the explosives on their body they made also autonomous decisions on how to maximise the damage potential. As al-Qaeda declared themselves as partly responsible for that bloody nightmare the attacks can be linked to the global Islamic terrorism.

The fourth case that has to be studied is the killing that happened on the 2th March 2011 at Frankfurt airport. ("Chronologie - Terroranschläge in Europa - Politik - Süddeutsche.de", n. d.) An Islamic motivated terrorist assassinated two US soldiers with deadly headshots and another two were seriously harmed. („Frankfurter Flughafen-Attentäter erhält lebenslange Haft", 2012) As the attacker tried to shoot the fifth soldier his pistol had a malfunction and he could be arrested by the security forces. („Frankfurter Flughafen-Attentäter erhält lebenslange Haft", 2012) The judge stated that Arid Uka was a perpetrator on his own and that he wanted to contribute to the global jihad with his act. („Frankfurter Flughafen-Attentäter erhält lebenslange Haft", 2012) This terrorist attack on German soil counts as the first Islamic terrorist attack that could not be prevented in Germany. („Frankfurter Flughafen-Attentäter erhält lebenslange Haft", 2012) As munitions for his attack he used a pistol and a knife that he used to attack the police forces after his pistol had a malfunction. („Schüsse am Frankfurter Flughafen", 2011) These weapons are small arms and can be fit into category number three. That is also the reason why the attacker could work on his own without a terror network behind him. Those small arms are easy to obtain and a long training process was not needed for him. But fortunately, the damage potential of those small arms is limited as it could be seen with a malfunctioning pistol. This airport strike could also be interpreted as a kind of global Islamic terrorism because the terrorist confessed himself to the global jihad in front of the court. („Frankfurter Flughafen-Attentäter erhält lebenslange Haft", 2012) This is the first case in the study where small firearms were used.

Furthermore the attacks of Anders Behring Breivik in Oslo on the 22th July 2011 have to be closer examined. („Timeline", 2016) He has planned and executed two different attacks on Norway, one in the city centre of Oslo and another one at an island called Utøya where members of the Norwegian Labour Party gathered. (Syse, 2014) His first target was the main governmental building of Norway in Oslo where the prime minister is working. (Syse, 2014) On Friday afternoon at 3:25 pm a 950 kg homemade fertilizer bomb blew up in a car parked near the governmental building placed there by Anders Breivik. (Syse, 2014) Luckily a lot of officials were on their summer vacation and only eight were killed by the bomb, it could have been way worse. (Syse, 2014) Around 200 people were injured by the blast of the big bomb and the explosion could be heard from over four miles away. (Syse, 2014) The bomb managed it even to set the governmental building on fire. (Syse, 2014) But this was only the first attack of Breivik that was thought to be a distraction from his even more lethal second strike. This bloodbath was planned in advance by Breivik and he was dressed up as a police officer fully armed in order to get to the island with the ferry with the justification to secure the island. (Syse, 2014) Immediately as he arrived there he began to shoot at innocent teenagers by using a Ruger Mini-14 semi-automatic rifle and a Glock pistol. („Norway is banning all semi-automatic guns, 10 years after Anders Breivik's attack", 2018) In this deadly one hour lasting firestorm Breivik slaughtered 69 adolescents and another 33 innocent youngsters were severely injured. (Syse, 2014) When a SWAT team arrived on the island Breivik surrendered to them without any resistance. (Syse, 2014) Afterwards Breivik confessed that he wanted to save Norway and western Europe from a Muslim invasion and that the labour party had to pay the price for it. (Syse, 2014) According to that he can be described as a nationalistic right-wing extremist who has turned into a lone acting terrorist. In order to examine the munitions of this bloody attack more closely both attacks have to be separately considered. The first attack was carried out by a very big homemade fertilizer bomb that qualifies itself for an improvised explosive device because it could be manufactured locally at the terrorists home. That means that the munition he used in his first attack is falling under category one, the explosives. In his second attack on the island Breivik used a pistol and a semi-automatic weapon for his lethal bloodbath. Those weapons are counting for the small firearms category, the third one. Because of the loose gun regulations it was easy to get them for Breivik and he was trained in handling them as a member of the hunting club. (Aspøy, 2011) This case is the first one in this research in what the terrorist combined two different categories of munitions in a big attack in order to maximise the damage potential.

In the next case a terrorist attacked the Jewish Museum in Brussel on May 24th 2014. („Chronologie - Terroranschläge in Europa - Politik - Süddeutsche.de", n. d.) The extremist used an AK-47 assault gun to slaughter 3 people and one employee of the museum was severely injured. („Jüdisches Museum in Brüssel", 2014) According to the investigators the gunman acted on his own and did a detailed planning before executing his strike. („Jüdisches Museum in Brüssel", 2014) Afterwards he fled by foot and could escape from the police. („Jüdisches Museum in Brüssel", 2014) But due to the good investigations made by the French police he could be arrested in Marseille one week later. (Lehnartz, 2014) The investigators found also out that the terrorist, Mohamed Merah, had connections to the Islamic state and his attack was antisemitic motivated. (Lehnartz, 2014) This bloody incident was clearly part of a global Islamic terrorism with a link to the big terror network of the Islamic state. Furthermore, the terrorist used an AK-47 for his attack and that weapon is without any doubt an automatic assault rifle. In conclusion, this type of munition is related to the automatic weapons in category four.

Evermore, the following series of incidents happened in Paris beginning with targeting the satire magazine Charlie Hebdo on the 7th of January 2015. („Chronologie - Terroranschläge in Europa - Politik - Süddeutsche.de", n. d.) The city of Paris was rocked by a series of attacks three days in a row. („Charlie Hebdo attack", 2015) It all began on the 7th of January when two gunman who were considered as brothers stormed the satire magazine Charlie Hebdo and managed to get access to the second floor of the office building. („Charlie Hebdo attack", 2015) The opened up the fire with a AK-47 and killed 11 people within the building after this deadly attack both terrorist could manage it to get away from the police by car. („Charlie Hebdo attack", 2015) One witness said that the terrorist said that they wanted to get revenge for the satiric drawing of the prophet Muhammad. („Charlie Hebdo attack", 2015) Both brothers were killed two days later in a police shootout. („Charlie Hebdo attack", 2015) But Paris could not get to calm down in this bloody series of terrorist attacks. On the next day, the 9th of January 2015, a lone gunman shot down a police officer and injured another man during the search for the responsible perpetrators for the attack of the satire magazine. („Charlie Hebdo attack", 2015) The gunman was very heavily armed by a machine-gun and the police could confirm that this assassination was linked to the attacks on the previous day. („Charlie Hebdo attack", 2015) But the terrorist was able to flee another time. („Charlie Hebdo attack", 2015) The next day, on the 9th of January another incident happened. While the police had a standoff with both attackers of Charlie Hebdo another terrorist took hostages in a kosher supermarket in Paris in order to blackmail the police to free both terrorists of Charlie Hebdo. („Charlie Hebdo attack", 2015) Fortunately, the police could end the siege of the supermarket and killed the third terrorist and freed the hostages. („Charlie Hebdo attack", 2015) Despite their efforts the terrorist in the supermarket had already killed four people by using a TT pistol and a vz. 58 submachine gun. („Charlie Hebdo attack", 2015) But all attacks of this horrible series have one thing in common, they are all definitely motivated by the global Islamic terrorism. To categorise the used munitions, it is necessary to take a separate look at all three incidents and count the firearms of each attack once. In the first attack on the Charlie Hebdo building the terrorists used again the AK-47 as an assault rifle because of its reliability and high availability. It is classified as an automatic weapon. It has to be counted once for the fourth category. In the second incident the gunman was armed with a machine gun and that counts one time more for the fourth category of automatic weapons. The hostage taker of the supermarket was equipped with a TT pistol and vz. 58 submachine gun. Both are counting as small firearms of category number three. To put it into a nutshell, automatic weapons were used in two attacks and small firearms in the last attack.

The following incident happened in Copenhagen on the 14th of February 2015. („Chronologie - Terroranschläge in Europa - Politik - Süddeutsche.de", n. d.) The attacker stormed a café where people were discussing about free speech with a M/95 rifle and opened up the fire immediately, killing one man and wounded three police officers. („Politi", 2015) Overnight the terrorist killed a Jewish person in front of a synagogue. („‚Copenhagen gunman' shot by police", 2015) On the morning of the 15th of February 2015 it came to a lethal standoff with the police and the terrorist was shot dead while pulling out his gun. („‚Copenhagen gunman' shot by police", 2015) Afterwards the investigators were not sure what motives Omar Abdel Hamid El-Hussein had but they assumed a political reason behind it. („‚Copenhagen gunman' shot by police", 2015) His M/95 automatic rifle can be classified as an assault rifle in category four, the automatic weapons.

At least, the focus should be moved now on one of the most lethal terroristic attacks that happened in Europe. It hit Paris again in another strike on the 15th of November 2015. („Chronologie - Terroranschläge in Europa - Politik - Süddeutsche.de", n.d.) This series of attacks have to be looked at separately. In total, 130 people were killed and nearly 700 more were injured. („Paris attacks", 2015) The numbers alone are giving an idea how enormous and deadly those attacks were. The first assault happened around 9:20 pm at the Stade de France. („Paris attacks", 2015) A suicide bomber wearing a belt of explosives wanted to get inside the stadium but was prevented from getting in by the security. („Paris attacks", 2015) Immediately he pulled back and blew himself up killing one pedestrian. („Frankreich vs Deutschland 2:0 - Zwei Explosionen während des Spiels 13.11.2015 - YouTube", 2015) Following the first detonation another two suicide bombers wearing an identical explosive vest blew themselves up at a different entrance and in a fast food court near the stadium. („Frankreich vs Deutschland 2:0 - Zwei Explosionen während des Spiels 13.11.2015 - YouTube", 2015) A series of gun attacks followed the first explosion on Rue Alibert. („Paris attacks", 2015) The attack starting around 9:25 pm hit restaurants and bars by using semi-automatic weapons. („Paris attacks", 2015) The restaurant Le Petit Cambodge was attacked first and 15 people were killed and 15 more were severely injured. („Paris attacks", 2015) In addition, some cafés were attacked nearby the restaurant and five were killed and eight were badly harmed. („Paris attacks", 2015) Some minutes afterwards another nearby Bar was attacked by two gunman killing 19 people and injuring nine more. („Paris attacks", 2015) The shootings at the restaurant were followed by another suicide bomber blowing himself up at Boulevard Voltaire around 9:40 pm. („Paris attacks", 2015) Fortunately this explosion killed no one but one person was still heavily injured. („Paris attacks", 2015) The climax of this bloody tragedy was marked by the attacks on the Bataclan concert hall. It started at 9:40 pm with three gunmen breaking into the fully booked concert hall and opening up the fire by using Kalashnikov assault rifles taking down 98 people. („Paris attacks", 2015) Around one hundred other innocent people were taken into hospital. („Paris attacks", 2015) At 0:20 am a special unit team stormed the hall and killed one of the terrorist by detonating his explosive belt and the other two blew themselves up. („Paris attacks", 2015) This strike is one of the worst happening in Europe and it was largely planned in detail by the terror network of the Islamic State (ISIS). („Who were the Paris attackers?", 2016) For sure this attack can be categorised as an global Islamic terrorism to create an constant atmosphere of war. But ISIS had as well another strategic aim in mind. The terror network wanted to force president Hollande to withdraw his French soldiers from the war in Syria. Finally, the munitions that were used in this terrifying attack have to be closer examined and categorised. The first attack on the stadium was done by suicide bombers wearing explosives. They are counting to category nine. In the second assault on the bars the terrorist used semi-automatic rifles and those are counting once to the small firearms category, number three. In the last attack on the Bataclan concert hall the attackers used automatic assault rifles of the type Kalashnikov as well as explosive belts. Those weapons are counting once for the category number nine and once for number four. It needs to be pointed out that the terrorists used a diversified spectrum of munitions in order to deal as much damage as possible.

4. Did the terrorists in Europe change their arsenal?

Firstly, in order to assess if the terrorists changed their munitions since the year 2000 a statistic is needed how often a category was used in one assault each.

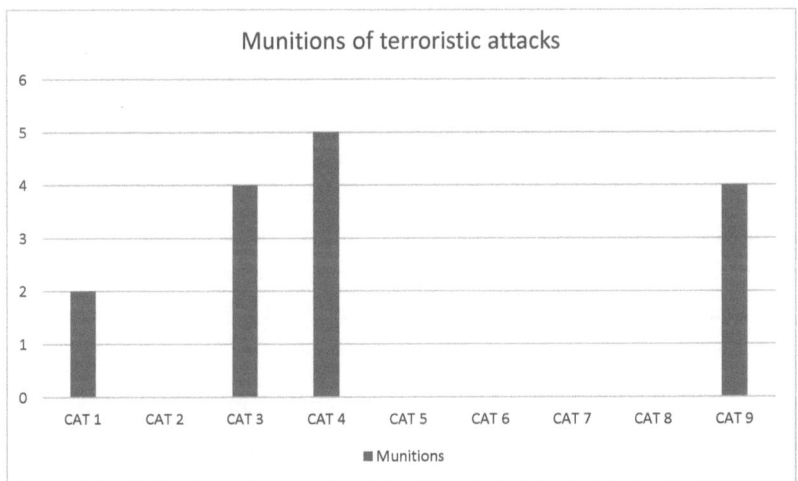

This diagram depicts how often each category of munitions was used in one terrorist attack. Firstly, it is eye-catching that none of the terrorists used CAT 2, CAT 5, CAT 6, CAT 7, and CAT 8. It needs to be closer examined why they didn´t use the munitions of those categories. Category 2, ambushes and assassinations were not used for terroristic purpose. That might be an indicator that the damage potential is limited to one person for the terrorists and the targets might be protected very good as well. It also needs a lot of patience and planning in order to secure the assassination. It is also very costly and the assassins have to be trained very well. That might be a reason for the terrorists not to use the munitions of category 2 anymore. For terrorists who are motivated by the global Islamic terrorism this method is also contra productive because the target group is limited to a small number of important people and it doesn´t create a constant climate of war. Furthermore, category five, the portable rocket launchers, wasn´t used as well for terroristic attacks. That could be explained that their availability in a region with stable institutions and peace is not so good than in failing states like Somalia. The border patrol might also prohibit such heavy war weapons to get into the EU. In addition, the terrorists need to be trained in operating such complex weapons and they have to assemble them. They have also just a limited use in urban regions. It is also extraordinary that no aerial hijackings were done by terrorist since the year 2000 in the European region. That can be explained by the high security standards at the airports as well as on board of the airplane. It is not possible to smuggle any weapon on board and the air forces are also allowed to shoot down a hijacked airplane in order to prevent more damage. It is also very risky for terrorists to get uncovered while planning it and the damage potential is limited as well to only the passengers on the airplane. It needs also to be pointed out that no big cyber attacks and sabotages happened that would possibly kill a lot of people. A possible explanation could be that the terrorists would need a lot of highly skilled IT experts as well as the technical equipment to do this. Also, the success rate would maybe not be so good because western countries might have a good cyber defence and launching an attack would be very costly. Fortunately, category eight, the weapons of mass destruction, wasn´t used until today for a terrorist attack on Europe. That's because they need to get their hands-on nuclear material and the terrorist organisation must have the facilities and the technical skill in order to build such a device. It is as well very costly and needs a lot of preparation and the terrorist are risking their own life during the assembling process as well.

It was showed what munitions the terrorists didn´t use for their attack. Now, the focus should be switched to what arms they really used in order to answer the posed research question from the beginning.

What munitions are terrorists in Europe using today and did they change since the beginning of the 21st century?

To begin with, it is noticeable that explosives from category one was used twice in the attacks and is one of the least used munitions. The explosives can be assembled pretty easily but the preparation takes very long. The terrorist have to deposit the explosives on the right place and they need to be triggered in the right time to deal the highest damage as possible. There is also the risk that the terrorists are getting uncovered and they also have to plan an escape route. They also need some technical skill in order to detonate the bomb with a trigger from a distance. Still, it is very dangerous and the damage can be extremely vast as it was shown. Still it is very extensive to plan such an attack. This kind of munitions is also more focused on accomplishing a strategic goal like the retreat of foreign troops. That explains, why the terrorists didn´t use them more often. Category nine and three were used in the same extend and often. In total both munitions were used in four cases. The small firearms are easy to handle for smaller terrorist groups or for a lone perpetrator. They are as well easy to get on the black market and very inexpensive. But still their damage potential is limited to killing a few of innocent people without a long phase of training and planning. That might explain why terrorists in Europe are using them frequently. The cases in which suicide bombers did the attack is also fairly high. The reasons for that might be the efficient way to deal a lot of damage to an unlimited number of people with low skills and effort. Terror networks are able to sacrifice their low skilled martyrs in order to spread their global Islamic terrorism. And because of the terrorist being able to make autonomous decisions with his ratio he can inflict the biggest damage possible. The explosives can also be assembled locally and the material can be bought at any hardware show what secures a high availability. Those are the reasons why they are so popular amongst European terrorists. But the most widespread munition of terrorists in Europe are the automatic weapons with a total number of five measured incidents. Those weapons are easy and inexpensive to get on the black market as well and they can be covered in an urban area. In addition, they have a high rate of fire and can deal a lot of harm in a short time. The psychological damage that they inflict is also horrible. Automatic weapons like the AK-47 are also very reliable when it comes to the attack and easy to handle. With those heavy weapons the terrorists can also challenge security forces that are equipped only with small firearms. That explains why automatic weapons are the favourite ones amongst European terrorists.

In conclusion, terrorists today are using mainly suicide bombers in a combination with small firearms and automatic weapons in order to maximise the damage potential and lower their own costs. To combine those categories make todays terroristic attacks extremely lethal and shocking for the European society. They didn´t change their arsenal completely in the 21st century but they are using now the most efficient and rational way to inflict the highest damage possible.

This conclusion also supports my hypothesis of the beginning as well.

If we know what arms the European extremists are using for their attacks nowadays beforehand, we can prevent those attacks better.

Now, the tendency of a terrorists arsenal is pointed out as combining multiple types of conventional munitions in one lethal attack. The anti-terror units can be trained how to deal better with a terrorist who is equipped with an assault rifle or what to do when an Islamic martyr is wearing an explosive belt before blowing himself up. They have to learn how to tackle those situations better. It could also help to introduce stronger gun regulation laws within the European community in order to prevent the terrorists from getting in-touch with automatic weapons and small firearms. Furthermore, the illicit trafficking of black-market weapons could be stronger monitored by the border patrol. In addition, big public gatherings should be guarded better by heavily armed security forces. Those measurements cannot stop completely the terrorists from attacking the inhabitants of Europe, but it would discourage them and reduce the number of killed innocent victims.

5. Literature

7/7 attacks: What happened that day? (2015, Juli 3). Abgerufen von https://www.bbc.com/news/uk-33253598

Aspøy, A. (2011, August 29). Skytternes taushet. Abgerufen 18. Januar 2019, von https://www.dagbladet.no/a/63593483

Champion, D., & Mattis, R. (2003). Terrorism, weapons of mass destruction and deterrence. *Criminal Justice Studies, 16*(1), 29–37. https://doi.org/10.1080/08884310309606

Charlie Hebdo attack: Three days of terror. (2015, Januar 14). Abgerufen von https://www.bbc.com/news/world-europe-30708237

Chronologie - Terroranschläge in Europa - Politik - Süddeutsche.de. (n.d.). Abgerufen 8. Januar 2019, von https://www.sueddeutsche.de/politik/chronologie-terroranschlaege-in-europa-1.1123846

Combs, C. C. (2017). *Terrorism in the Twenty-First Century* (Bd. Eighth edition). New York, NY: Routledge. Abgerufen von http://search.ebscohost.com/login.aspx?direct=true&db=nlebk&AN=1641420&site=ehost-live

„Copenhagen gunman" shot by police. (2015, Februar 15). Abgerufen von https://www.bbc.com/news/world-europe-31475803

De Masi, F. (2011). *The Enigma of the Suicide Bomber: A Psychoanalytic Essay*. London, UNITED KINGDOM: Routledge. Abgerufen von http://ebookcentral.proquest.com/lib/linne-ebooks/detail.action?docID=788050

Frankfurter Flughafen-Attentäter erhält lebenslange Haft. (2012). Abgerufen 17. Januar 2019, von https://www.tagesspiegel.de/gesellschaft/panorama/anschlag-auf-us-soldaten-frankfurter-flughafen-attentaeter-erhaelt-lebenslange-haft/6195912.html

Frankreich vs Deutschland 2:0 - Zwei Explosionen während des Spiels 13.11.2015 - YouTube. (2015, November 20). Abgerufen 19. Januar 2019, von https://www.youtube.com/watch?v=DWKXvQ24N8U

Istanbul rocked by double bombing. (2003, November 20). Abgerufen von http://news.bbc.co.uk/2/hi/europe/3222608.stm

Jenkins, B. M. (1978). INTERNATIONAL TERRORISM: Trends and Potentialities. *Journal of International Affairs, 32*(1), 115.

Jüdisches Museum in Brüssel: Polizei startet Großfahndung nach mutmaßlichem Attentäter. (2014). Abgerufen von https://www.faz.net/1.2956909

Lehnartz, S. (2014, Juni 1). 29-jähriger Franzose : Film-Geständnis des Brüsseler Terror-Attentäters. Abgerufen von https://www.welt.de/politik/ausland/article128616018/Film-Gestaendnis-des-Bruesseler-Terror-Attentaeters.html

Norway is banning all semi-automatic guns, 10 years after Anders Breivik's attack. (2018, Februar 28). Abgerufen 17. Januar 2019, von http://www.independent.co.uk/news/world/europe/norway-gun-ban-semi-automatic-weapons-anders-brevik-shooting-florida-school-massacre-a8232106.html

Paris attacks: What happened on the night. (2015, Dezember 9). Abgerufen von https://www.bbc.com/news/world-europe-34818994

Politi: Forsvarets automat-riffel brugt ved terror-angreb. (2015). Abgerufen 18. Januar 2019, von https://ekstrabladet.dk/nyheder/samfund/politi-forsvarets-automat-riffel-brugt-ved-terror-angreb/5444821

Ray, M. (2018). London bombings of 2005 | History, Facts, & Map. Abgerufen 17. Januar 2019, von https://www.britannica.com/event/London-bombings-of-2005

Schüsse am Frankfurter Flughafen: Attentäter gesteht Anschlag auf US-Soldaten. (2011, März 3). *Spiegel Online*. Abgerufen von http://www.spiegel.de/politik/deutschland/schuesse-am-frankfurter-flughafen-attentaeter-gesteht-anschlag-auf-us-soldaten-a-748843.html

Syse, A. (2014). Breivik – The Norwegian Terrorist Case. *Behavioral Sciences & the Law*, *32*(3), 389–407. https://doi.org/10.1002/bsl.2121

The Synagogue Bombings in Istanbul: (2003). Abgerufen 16. Januar 2019, von https://www.washingtoninstitute.org/policy-analysis/view/the-synagogue-bombings-in-istanbul-al-qaedas-new-front

The worst Islamist attack in European history. (2007, Oktober 31). *The Guardian*. Abgerufen von https://www.theguardian.com/world/2007/oct/31/spain

Timeline: Terror attacks in Europe. (2016). Abgerufen 8. Januar 2019, von https://www.usatoday.com/story/news/world/2016/03/22/timeline-terror-attacks-europe/82108892/

Who were the Paris attackers? (2016, April 27). Abgerufen von https://www.bbc.com/news/world-europe-34832512

Why has the AK-47 become the jihadi terrorist weapon of choice? | World news | The Guardian. (n. d.). Abgerufen 14. Januar 2019, von https://www.theguardian.com/world/2015/dec/29/why-jihadi-terrorists-swapped-suicide-belts-kalashnikov-ak-47s

YOUR KNOWLEDGE HAS VALUE